FROM ME TO US

(The Journey To A Successful Marriage)

Contact Information:

Email: pastorostandley@gmail.com
Website: www.wix.com/pastorostandleyministries

Printed in The United States of America

DEDICATION

I dedicate this book to my wonderful husband Apostle Dean Standley! In his strength I've become stronger as a woman. In his silence I've learned how to "study to be quiet." In his correction, I've learned humility and in his LOVE, I've learned that it's okay to BLOSSOM!
His LOVE for God and His time in worship to God has pushed me even deeper and for that I give God all the Praise! Dean is my friend, my lover, provider and protector; my life long partner in this journey to Heaven! As we always declare, "We are doing LIFE!"
I Love you Boo!

Your "Ride and Live" partner,
Mrs. Octavia Standley

Table of Content (Hers)

Table of Content (His)

Table of Content (From Me to US)

PREFACE

Let's just get straight to the point, more than likely you are picking up this book because something has gone awry in your marriage and you are either at your "wits end and on the verge of giving up" or you're determined to fight!
Better still, maybe you are single, not married, newly engaged and want to know everything you can to ensure your marriage survives. No matter the case, I am here to share with you some things that I have learned in marriage. Some things I learned through experience, others through the teaching, leading and instruction of God.

My desire is for you to open your heart and ears to receive. Not everything I'm going to say is going to "feel" good to the "what about me?" spirit in you but if you are truly invested in and want to see your marriage flourish, you will swallow the pill.

We are going to delve into some of the mindsets, attitudes and beliefs (good and bad) that many have developed over the course of their lives. Some of the things you've picked up along the way are the very things that have been toxic to and have damaged many of your relationships. Without intention, whether married or single, you may have carried excess baggage into your relationship yet you wonder why the "load seems so heavy."

Maybe you've developed some of the same mindsets, attitudes and beliefs that your mom and dad had in their marriage, and are finding out that they are not going to work in yours!

Marriage is a wonderful thing but believe me, it takes work! You're going to have to "DIE" to you! The "man/woman in the mirror" is going to have to make the adjustment from the mindset of one to the mindset of ONE!

It is at this point that I must reiterate my previous statement, *"if you are truly invested in and want to see your marriage flourish, you will swallow the pill."* The fight for your marriage is worth it!

God's Love and Mine,
Octavia Standley

INTRODUCTION

If the average person (whether male or female) would be honest, they would admit that at the moment of disagreement "self-preservation," and "self-interest" kicks in.
In our red angry faces, stiffened posture, hands on the hips, finger pointing stances we are prepared to defend our ideology, principles, thoughts and beliefs to the death; even the death of a relationship or marriage! Obviously if you think its right it must be right, correct?

May I submit to you for your consideration that maybe, just maybe this initial reaction to disagreement may just be the cause of many separations and divorce? While I'm at it, might I further suggest that if you just "die" *(I'll explain this later)* there is a great possibility that you can save your marriage and rekindle the fire you once had?

Through my own marital experiences and by counseling numerous other married couples, I've found that the "Key" to a happy marriage, the "Key" to rekindling the fires of passion that have fizzled, is tucked safely in the bible, you only need to go find it and apply it.

The "Key" is so simple to use and at the same time so hard to apply. A successful marriage all hinges on.........

DYING TO SELF!

From Genesis to Revelation, the Bible gives us such beautiful scriptures on marriage and such stern warnings on what things should not happen within the confines of marriage. Once married, "I" and "Me" go out the window! It's now "We" and "Us," remember, the two have now become ONE!

In marriage there is no longer any separation, no longer any room for selfishness and there certainly isn't any room for you to be self-centered! What's good for ME must now evolve into what's good for US! Love will make you do that!

Speaking of Love, 1 Corinthians chapter 13 is one of my favorite passages of scriptures when I talk to married couples. We often read it and apply it to everything but marriage. In this book we will look at it from just a little different angle.
Its time now to go a little bit deeper into this process of "dying" to self!

Let's start this Journey together as we learn how to go from Me to US!

The Journey To US Begins...

Dolls and Dreams
(Her)

I once heard a man of God (*Bishop Ishmael Charles*) say that the word dream stood for **D**ivine **R**evealed **E**vent **A**waiting **M**anifestation. How appropriate that is for this section on Dolls and Dreams.

Many girls had dolls when they were young. We named our dolls, played with our dolls, and carried our dolls with us wherever we went. Our dolls were our babies, we changed their diapers, we found them "boyfriends" (usually a green army man) and made them play house. Our dolls got "married," cooked dinner, had tea parties and had "babies" of their own. Our dolls even "owned" houses and cars and went to work.

We saw ourselves in our dolls. We had dreams of getting married, becoming a wife, having children, a house and car, living the perfect "Suburbian" life, complete with a husband who had a Fortune 500 job and who loved us with a faithful love.

We had a DREAM, a Divine Revealed Event Awaiting Manifestation! It was wired into our DNA from the beginning of time to be a help meet, lover, and friend. One who walks alongside her husband helping him to bring his vision for the family to pass!

We are the incubators; so to speak, of life that receives, multiplies and brings forth more than what was originally deposited in us.

For example, the bible declares that we are to be *fruitful and multiply,* there's no multiplying without FEMALE so without us, there would be no more us! We are the essential piece and component (besides God) to a man's life that will cause his vision to go from Dream to Reality. Why do I say that? The bible declares that a "*man who finds a wife finds a **good thing** and **obtains FAVOR** from the Lord.*" YOU bring favor, YOU are a good thing! In our spirits as little girls, we were putting into action, through our dolls, the **D.R.E.A.M** that was already hard wired in us by God!

Our dolls were our practice, our lives are the MANIFESTATION!

So as you can see ladies, you have been the "center of attention" from the very beginning. The "very good thing" that God spoke of after man's creation.

Although this is a great thing, the problem comes in when some of us don't quite make the transition from the mindset of ME once we become an US, but we'll get into that just a little bit later.....

Action Hero
(Him)

G.I. Joe with the "Kung-Fu" Grip (*produced by Hasbro)* was an all-time favorite of young men all around the world! This action hero spoke to the natural warrior, defender and protector hard wired into men.

With these action hero's you could find young men "parachuting" off of their bunk beds, hiding in the closet, throwing "grenades" at their enemies (usually their sisters dolls and teddy bears) and sneaking behind enemy lines (their sisters bed room) gathering Intel.

From cowboys to army men, super heroes to wrestlers, young men too were living out a D.R.E.A.M (Divine Revealed Event Awaiting Manifestation.) How many of our young men have imagined themselves saving the day, the world, and the damsel in distress? How many of them have secretly desired her sweet kiss of admiration and the parade that was sure to be held for them due to their heroic deeds? I'm sure it's more than the world will ever know. Those types of "dreams" are secretly hidden in the well-guarded vault of the male ego.

Fast forward to the first time you as a young male, somewhere between the ages of 5-7, came to moms rescue as you located her lost ring and were rewarded with five dollars and a kiss! Wow....you felt like a hero!
Or what about the first girl you helped find her lost puppy or defended from a bully who was pushing her.

Her smile literally melted your heart (*of course she'd never know it*) and you walked away "like a boss" not looking back over your shoulder but knowing full well she was watching you in admiration!

You only did what you were hard wired by God to do!

In Genesis 2 when God formed the animals from the dust of the ground, He brought those animals to Adam to name and whatever name that Adam gave to the animal, THAT was its name! Talk about a BOSS! Just like the first man Adam, men all over the world both young and old have been presented with problems that needed solving and like the men of dominion, power and authority that they were created to be, they learned to subdue those things like a "Boss!"

Nothing is wrong with that, it is as it should be, however.... if a "boss" is not careful; a boss will only look out for its own interest (...*that woman that Thou gave me*), and leave others high and dry.

Even the "boss" has to learn to shift his mindset from ME to US! But as I said before, we'll dig into that just a little bit later...

Matured and Ready to Marry
First boyfriend
(Her)

Matured according to *The Free Dictionary* is defined as "having or showing characteristics, such as, patience and prudence, considered typical of well-balanced adulthood: mature for her age.

Vocabulary.com defines matured as "something that's fully developed, at its peak of being alive and mature.

In a December 19, 2013 publication of *Cerebral Cortex,* a study done by scientists at New Castle University in the UK concluded that females as a whole mature faster in certain areas such as cognition and emotions due to the fact that girls tend to optimize brain connections earlier than boys.

The reasoning for this is a process called "pruning." in a nutshell it means that in a child's early development the brain is taking in so much information from outside stimuli that its neurons and connections and folding of the brains surface are in excess of what's actually needed.

So "pruning" of the brain happens to make the brain more refined and efficient. In essence, your brain deletes what it doesn't need therefore maturing in the areas most often used. This "streamlining" so to speak happens at a faster rate with girls. Young men, unfortunately undergo this "streamlining" at a much slower rate.

With that understanding in mind, we can see why young teenage girls have already declared her first crush her "husband." She is already looking forward to the day where her developing or already developed body will carry her "boo's" or her "bae's" baby!

She already knows that she is to be the ONLY one; no other girl can have her man! He must be there to carry her books, put his arm around her as they walk down the hallways, and walk her to her locker! She is the ONLY one to wear his Letterman's jacket so that ALL know that he belongs to her!

No longer is she thinking about the doll that used to hold her dreams, she has now "matured" into a "woman" capable of an "adult" relationship. She no longer has times for the "games" that kids play. She's thinking future. Her brain has already pruned out most of the "little girls fantasy" she only has time for reality!

Don't get me wrong, she will always be daddy's little girl but to her "man," don't get it twisted, she's ALL woman! All day long she scribbles her "new name" on her folders and notebooks, *"Mrs. John Doe, I luv John Doe, 2 hearts 2gether 4-ever"* and all the little gushy stuff that we use to write!

She no longer gets excited by the green army man or the G.I Joe with the Kung-Fu grip walking alongside her doll; she only has eyes for the captain of the football or basketball team!

While picking out her homecoming and/or prom dress, she is imaging her wedding gown! The pictures taken at the dance, just a foreshadow of the wedding that is sure to come.

She already sees them going to the same college, living in an apartment together and walking off into "Happily Ever After" upon college graduation!

Oh yes, she has it all worked out according her time table and schedule. Its picture perfect!! Or is it?

You have already worked your life out and poor little "Bae," who is clearly clueless to your "future" plans, doesn't even have a say in the matter!

This lone decision making process more often than not finds its way into many marriages (*Remember, it was Eve who decided it was best that they eat of the forbidden fruit...*) and even more often, results in disaster!

Again, the saga of ME vs. US continues!

First Girlfriend
(Him)

I conducted a survey (very informal, just a few men) and I asked them how they met their very first girlfriend? From elementary school to high school the answers were pretty much the same...they were introduced to their girlfriends via sisters, cousins or friends. Either they would ask for the "hook up" or their male friends would edge them on and say "man, you should date her!" thus their stories began!

This seems to be so much different from the approach of the little girls, the little girls, whose brains are already firing at a faster rate. The little girls saw, came and conquered. They knew what they wanted and they instinctively knew how to get it.

Young men however, may or may not have known what they wanted and had to be goaded into being a boyfriend, drawn into being a boyfriend or even told "you're my boyfriend!" Remember, they are still going through the "pruning" process and haven't quite caught up with the faster maturation rate of the little girls!

Now that they have been goaded, drawn in or told, the young men naturally step into an awkward yet hard wired position of protector, defender, and hero. He's enjoying the moment while the young lady is thinking ahead.

He's enjoying video games, high school sports, punching other boys until they develop a "frog" in their arms and wondering where his next meal is going to come from!

He's enjoying the "alpha male" role or maybe he's the guy in the corner that hasn't yet (*and probably won't until he grows out of his pimples and retainer*) caught the attention of a little girl. Either way, he's living in the NOW while young girls have already shifted to future!

More than likely, he's only living for that "*Now I'm a man*" moment. You know that moment; that first kiss, first feel, that first run to "second or third base." and if he makes it to "home plate" Woo-hoo!!! he KNOWS he's the man then!

And while he's having a locker room blow by blow detailed (*truth or not*) bragging session about how he "got that," his girlfriend's heart has already settled into the fact that after that intimate encounter, "he's most certainly mine now."

In most instances, the two will date for a while after the "home plate" experience but as in almost survey I conducted, the young men were eventually ready to move on to greener pastures having "conquered" the Land of You.

It's not that they are horrible people; it's just that they are natural born pursuers and are still going through the brains "pruning" process. They haven't reached the "maturity level" in cognition and emotions, that the young women have so saying "I Love you" to "score" doesn't seem all that wrong to them. Giving you their Letterman jacket in exchange for a "feel" is worth it to them.

But, once they have "conquered the land" I believe something happens in their brains. It is my belief (*and I most certainly could be wrong*) that the fear of rejection and the fear of "poor performance" has now become a thing of the past and due to the innate desire to pursue and conquer, they move on to the next girlfriend, sometimes never looking back.

The spirit of "Me" has once again won.

Disclaimer please don't get me wrong, I know that there are many awesome "we dated all through high school and college" marriage stories out there! I know a few of them myself. But for the most part, this is the typical high school experience. And despite this, many still move on to live great and productive lives.

The Flirt
(Her)
Flirt (Verb)
Behave as though attracted to or trying to attract someone, but for amusement rather than with serious intentions.

Merriam-Webster Dictionary defines flirt as: to behave in a way that shows a sexual attraction for someone but is not meant to be taken seriously.

Ha! Yeah right! When a woman flirts, she means it! That little "flirty" stuff women do at their favorite restaurant to get a discount or bigger portion or that "cute" little smile she does for the clerk at the convenience store to get that fountain drink for free, that's not flirting, that's being coy.

No, when a woman flirts (bats her lashes, catches a man's eye and looks away) she wants you to know that she's interested and available and wants you to "catch" her subtle or not so subtle hint.

Please know, that the moment a woman walks into a classroom, board meeting, gas station, library, church, lounge, sports arena, etc....her antenna are already up and activated. Without you knowing, she knows if you're a "waste of her time," a potential, the alpha male or a scrub. We don't want no scrubs (*song by TLC*), you can't get no love from us!

Once a woman decides you're worth a little more investigating, the flirting begins.

It always starts with a little light conversation, followed by a strategically placed hand on the arm or shoulder as she laughs at something her intended says. She will either be "caught" at this stage or she will with class excuse herself from the conversation, hoping to find someone just a little more interesting.

So the journey of see, flirt, captivate begins again until at last she finds what she's looking for and then it's on! If she knows she'll probably see you again, you may or may not get her number the first time (*we gotta keep you coming back for more*) but eventually there will be an exchange of business card or the tap-tap-tapping of numbers being entered into her intendeds' cell phone.

If all goes according to her plans (*remember, her "pruned" brain has already matured in cognition and emotions so she's ready to settle down*), she will soon be having thoughts of whirlwind dating, beautiful courtship, and an amazing wedding ceremony and marriage.

The problem with flirting is that it's always done with ulterior motive and if the intended doesn't act right, they will be quickly dropped as the woman moves on to greener pastures. She doesn't have time for games, she ready for marriage.

Isaiah 3:16 (NIV) reads, The LORD says, "The women of Zion are haughty, walking along with outstretched necks, **flirting** with their eyes, strutting along with swaying hips, with ornaments jingling on their ankles.

Oh we women know how to work it! Flirting is right up our alley! If we get the man's attention, more than likely we get the man!

I must issue a warning here. Although I believe it is OK to let a man know that you are interested too, I'm still a firm believer in the fact that a man does the pursuing and we as women CHOOSE.

The scripture says, a ***man that finds***...that means he does the pursuing but somehow in this modern society we have decided that *"men move too slow," "there's not enough men to go around so I better get mine," "I'm going to propose to him because its taking him to long to propose to me."* this type of thinking is OUT OF ORDER.

So, to fulfill our desires and with our future in mind many women use the laced with motive flirting technique to secure our ultimate destination, marital bliss.

Flirting is about YOU and your quest for an US. The problem is, if you don't destroy the "flirt" in you, it will bring division or even worse, divorce into your marriage. The "Flirt" in your ME season has to DIE before you should ever consider becoming an US!

Older and Ready To Ogle!
(Him)

Something one of my big brothers in the spirit said to me will always stick with me. He said this in the context of a ministry we were doing. He said, "If I went back into the world, I would be dangerous." I asked him what he meant by that and he continued to explain, "I can discern the hurting, emotionally broken and wounded women. They would be easy prey." and it hit me like a ton of bricks, many women out there have fallen victim to the "eye" that can see.

To Ogle (***Free Dictionary definition***) means to *look or stare at, especially in a desirous manner. A sustained look or stare.* It also means (***Dictionary.com***) *to look at amorously, flirtatiously, or impertinently.*

Statics show that women are ready to marry at an earlier age than men. I believe this has something to do with the "pruning" of the brain and the faster maturation rate of women and what was hard wired into us from the beginning.

Men it seems are well aware that they are outnumbered by women and although others may push for them to "marry" they are more likely to wait until it feels right for them. This may cause quite a bit of heart break for those women who happen to be a part of their "decision process" but until they are ready to "settle down" most men can't or won't be forced into marriage.

I believe in our day and time, the following scripture clearly shows why men in their 20's even up to early 30's are in no rush to say "I Do."

Isaiah 4:1 (KJV) reads, *"And in that day seven women shall take hold of one man, saying, We will eat our own bread, and wear our own apparel: only let us be called by thy name, to take away our reproach."*

Not trying to step on any toes or hurt any feelings but in a day where women are throwing themselves at men, dressing to reveal all their assets, cooking, cleaning, providing a warm bed and good loving (*which is out of order! Sexual intimacy is for the Marriage bed*), why would a man rush to put a ring on it?

According to Isaiah 4:1, it appears as if women are running to the altar of marriage, even if it means taking care of their own needs, while men are still perusing the "aisles."

Yes, they may be older and yes, they may have careers and businesses on a successful track but statics show that until about the age of 30 or so, "Boys, they wanna have fun!" they wanna look, they wanna handle, they wanna touch BUT they may not purchase.

Let me put it in terms that are even clearer. When a person does a taste test for cake for example, they may take a slice of and partake of several different cakes before they finally decide, "THIS is the ONE I want to purchase!" although the other cakes are far from nasty, it's something about the taste and texture of the chosen cake that makes the buyer decide to purchase.

Women you must understand that men are pursuers, even hunters if you will. They like to "spy out" their target, get a good eye and feel for their "target" and then pursue and overtake their "target." If you make the pursuit too easy, you may just be a "taste test" but, if you make them work for your attention (*meaning you know your value*) you cause them to go into overdrive trying to catch you!

Hear me; I am in no way advocating that it is OK to "Look, handle and touch" with no intent to purchase. This still points to looking out for Numero Uno, the ME mentality that hasn't yet bought into the US....

Letting Him Catch Me
(Her)

Men let me bust your bubbles real quick, your "skill" didn't get her; she LET YOU catch her! She knows exactly what she's looking for and she knows how to get it. She is skilled and tactical enough to set up the "game" in such a manner that you THINK your "surprise attack" overtook her but in actuality you fell into her well camouflaged trap.

Like the lioness who releases hormones into the wind for her intended to catch a whiff of, so too does the woman. It's called pheromones. Pheromones according to *Medical News Today* are chemicals animals produce which changes the behavior of another animal of the same species. They induce activity in other individuals, such as sexual arousal.

From the natural chemicals produced in our bodies to the perfumes and lotions we rub on our skin, the "fragrance of the woman" has been "pulling" men in since the beginning of time.

In nature the female of many species has their eyes and hearts set upon the strongest, most colorful, tallest and fiercest of their kind. They are looking for natural born protectors, the "leader of the pack" the male who will produce the strongest litter, and provide the safest habitat. They look for the male with stamina, resilience and intellect, a male with this combination has what it takes to get her!

As I stated before when she walks in the room, her antenna has already pointed to you. Through her subtle yet strategic movements, tone of voice and laughter, she leads you to believe that you are the most interesting man in the room (*you just might be*) and that your particular brand of "charm" pulled her in. If only that were true....

She set you up for the mark the moment she laid eyes on you! You became a participant in a "game" you knew nothing about. As a lioness rubs her body against the male making her intentions known , so the woman "accidentally" bumps into her intended "embarrassed" by the contact and like the chivalrous man that you are, you come to her rescue and help steady her so she doesn't "fall."

Now you've become the hero and like all hero's you were rewarded. You stroll out of the party, store, club, church or meeting feeling like your good looks and charm couldn't be resisted, when the truth is.....you've just been had!

The season of ME is almost over for you, and you don't even have a clue! You're well on your way to becoming an US!

As a reminder gentlemen, you didn't catch her; she let herself get caught.

***Ladies! NOW HEAR THIS! It does not take long for a man to decide what it is that he wants! Please know that if he hasn't made a move towards marriage and you've been in a relationship longer than 2 years you're probably an option but not his number one draft pick!

When God brought Eve to Adam, that man instantly knew, "This is bone of my bone and flesh of my flesh!" when Isaac saw Rebecca he was done for! When Jacob saw Rachel, this man became stronger than an ox and rolled back a boulder so that her flock could get something to drink! These men KNEW what they wanted and they did what was necessary to get it! Ladies, when a man wants you, he'll move heaven and hell to get you! There's no plan b and no other option! If there's still a linger, its a great possibility there will be no ring on your finger! Don't be the "consolation prize!" ***

She Fell For Your Bait *(cars, clothes and collections)*
(Him)

As an avid fisher woman, I understand the necessity of using the right bait. For instance, the bait I use for catfish (*who will eat almost anything*) is different from the bait that I would use to catch Bass. I can catch catfish from the land but for Mako shark and Swordfish (*both of which I really enjoy*) I can only get to in a boat built to handle the waves of the sea and I have to have the proper gear, equipment, poles and bait to get them (*they are no easy win! They put up a fight!*).

Men use "bait" too. From their cars to their clothes, cash to credit, all these different forms of "bait" have been used to pull in their "prize fish."

It doesn't matter if it's his friends car he's driving when he pulls you in or that fat bank roll you saw him pull out of his pocket as he paid for his food (*not knowing that it was ALL about to be gone once he paid his child support and other bills.*) None of that matters to him, all he knows is that his "bait" has caught you hook, line and sinker!

Sadly (*because they don't know their worth*), there are some "catfish" out there who will be caught by "hot dogs, corn, worms, liver, etc..." women who can be easily lured by one simple compliment, a hamburger at the local restaurant, and a movie complete with all the trimmings; large popcorn, drink, nacho's and candy (you know how expensive that can be!) This is land fishing. This doesn't require much effort, just some string a hook and some type of bait. It just has to look appealing for a catfish to bite.

Women please don't get mad at me, I'm only saying what we in our "knower" fear to be true but won't express out loud. I must admit...earlier in my life, before I knew my worth, I fell for the "catfish bait" too.

I can hear some of you saying, *"It's going to take more than that to get me!"* Well maybe you've been caught by the man who doesn't mind fishing in the local lake which requires a little more effort. He has to at least have his own boat or can afford to rent a boat. He has to be able to fuel his boat and lastly he has to have the gear, poles and bait to launch out. Maybe you are the Bass and require a more delicate lure for your palate.

Maybe the "fine dining" (*Cheesecake Factory, Red Lobster, etc...*) is what was used to get you. He gets you manicures and pedicures, massages at the local parlor and gets your hair done! You don't just watch movies, you go to the one with the recliners and servers that bring you your dinner (*far be it for you to stand in a line, order and carry your food like the others*)! He constantly feeds your ego by telling you how beautiful you are (*this is called "pitching and flipping" in the fishing world. Putting out just enough line to snag you.*) You guys go for walks in the park and even mini-vacations. He treats you like a lady and with his rented BMW, borrowed clothes and money (*or it could all be his*), he "Hooks" you and reels you in!

Then there are those women who know who they are and what they're worth. They too can be "caught" but a man has to put in WORK to get them!

This is what's called "Deep Sea Fishing" the ordinary, everyday fishing equipment that you buy at the local super center just won't do!

You have to carry "weight" when going after a swordfish! They are very smart, they are "deep" (*living 2000 ft. below the sea surface*) and aren't easily lured by "dangling bait." to get a "Swordfish" you can't just have a job, you must equal or better her Position! She's corporate, she's savvy, she's an intellectual and she's not easily persuaded. She's a Pastor, Public or Motivational Speaker, Doctor, Dentist or CEO. This woman has put in too much time, sweat and energy to just give herself to the first piece of bait dangled in her face.

Those men fishing for this type of women MUST have "properly prepared bait." Career, Luxury Vehicle, 401K, Great credit, Beautiful Home, Faithful, and be a Lover and Friend.
Fishing for "Swordfish" in the spirit arena requires a PURE, TRUE LOVE for God, faithfulness to both God and woman, a passion for the will of God and a hunger for souls to be saved. He has to devour the Word of God and be able to cover, wash and protect his woman!
In this arena the man too must have his own, which shows the ability to be a great steward of the things that God has given him. Career, car, home and a Vision, are all a must to "catch" a woman in the spirit.
A man has to be willing to sit in the "Fight Chair" (*a chair used to pull in big game fish such as Swordfish*) and fight for her Love.

She's not an easy win because she's not into games. She recognizes the "real" and only the "real" can reel her in!
Whether "Catfish," "Bass," or "'Swordfish" these women are of all ethnicity and age range. If a man really desires a mate he only need dangle the right bait!

You dangled, she bit; now what?

***Gentlemen! NOW HEAR THIS! It does not take long for you to decide what you want! If you KNOW you're not going to make a move towards marriage and you've been in a relationship longer than 2 years quit stringing her along! Stringing her along is selfish and all about you! If you're still "fishing" let her off the hook and allow her to be found by a man who is LOOKING FOR A WIFE and not just an option!

When God brought Eve to Adam, that man instantly knew, "This is bone of my bone and flesh of my flesh!" When Isaac saw Rebecca he was done for! When Jacob saw Rachel, this man became stronger than an ox and rolled back a boulder so that her flock could get something to drink! These men KNEW what they wanted and they did what was necessary to get it! Gentlemen, if you're not ready to move heaven and hell for her, if you still have a plan b, if there's still a linger, and you KNOW you're not going to put a ring on her finger (at least anytime soon) don't string her along! No woman wants to be the "consolation prize!" ***

Wifey Material
(Her)

His "bait" mesmerized you so you bit. You allowed him to "catch" you and reel you in. It's now time for him to take you home; you're the "fish" that didn't get away!

The dating has now commenced! He's wining and dining you. You guys fall asleep on the phone like high school kids. He's brought you to his home, introduced you to his boys, allowed you to meet his children (*he's met yours*) and now he wants to take you home to Moms, you know in your heart this man is serious about a future with you, after-all, he's now calling you "Wifey."

A word of caution this point in a relationship can be very tricky if all aren't on the same page! While she's thinking the next step is marriage (from Me to US), he may be thinking I love this girl, she's cool; I like being around her, we can go on like this forever (this "us" is good enough for me)! Many hearts and lives have been broken and fractured at this point in courtship. The woman (*or man*) may be dreaming of a future life complete with marriage and home, 2.5 kids and a dog; while the other is thinking, "This is my MVP" the most valuable player on my team. The problem with this is that once quite a bit of time has passed and the relationship seems as if it will progress no further, tension begins to replace the "tranquility," ultimatums are subtly (*and sometimes not so subtle*) made and a dark cloud of separation looms heavily over the relationship.

If no forward movement is made, couples eventually find themselves at an impasse and go their separate ways. This separation not only brings heartache to the man and woman but the children and family members who have been involved with the year's long relationship. "Fortified" hearts and calloused attitudes begin to develop in both male and female, making it even harder for the next person to get in. That's why it is important to have clear understanding of what each person is looking for in the relationship and what outcome they desire to see. Women make sure you're not giving "Wifey" benefits to a man who although he loves you, has only placed you at the level of MVP!***

(Back to the story)

Like a wife you fix him dinner, wash his clothes, manage his business affairs and watch his children for him as he hangs with the boys! There's no ring or promise of a marriage but your D.R.E.A.M refuses to die! So as good women and "wifey's" do, you pray for him, are understanding of his attitudes and willing to put up with some "red flags" and warnings because you are "Wifey" and a good wife stands by her man, right?

You are "All In" at this point. No other man catches your eye no matter the "bait" they dangle! You are faithful just the way you want your "hubby" to be faithful and cheating is not in your vocabulary! You are a "wife" for life and by the way he handles you, treats you, loves on you and presents you, you know that he knows this too!

You are "Wifey" material, any man can see that! You are a good woman who handles her business and handles it well!

His mom loves you, his kids adore you, and his friends even respect what you guys have! Oh yes! You are "Wifey" material! It's apparent to all! Unfortunately, he hasn't quite made that commitment yet. Yes, you are wonderful and have all the right attributes and characteristics of a great wife; however the title "wifey" is just that, a title. You're his MVP, a most valuable and needed member of his team. You are everything he desires so why mess up a good thing with a ring?

***Women, let me help you with something, AIN'T NOTHING CUTE ABOUT THE WORD "WIFEY!" You want to know why there is a "Y" behind Wife... because any man calling you "wifey" is still asking "Y" move on. He's comfortable with your current relationship and sees no need to take the next step! If you want to stay an option and not continue on the road to wedded bliss, stay a "wifey." those of you who know you are WIFE material......

The Journey to US continues....

My MVP
(Him)

She's tricked you into believing that your "bait" was so mesmerizing that she had to bite. She played hard to get but eventually allowed you to "catch" her and reel her in. It's now time to take her home and tell the story of the "fish" that didn't get away!

The dating has now commenced! You're whining and dining her. You guys fall asleep on the phone like high school kids. You've brought her to your home, introduced her to your boys, allowed her to meet your children and now you're taking her home to Moms! You love this woman! She's your MVP! You're even calling her "Wifey!" In your mind, it can't get any better than this!

A word of caution this point in a relationship can be very tricky if all aren't on the same page! While he's thinking, "This is my MVP" the most valuable player on my team! I like being around her, we can go on like this forever (this "us" is good enough for me)!
She's thinking marriage (from Me to US), dreaming of a future life complete with marriage, home, 2.5 kids and a dog.
The problem with this is that once quite a bit of time has passed and the relationship seems as if it will progress no further, tension begins to replace the "tranquility," ultimatums are subtly (*and sometimes not so subtle*) made and a dark cloud of separation looms heavily over the relationship. Many hearts and lives have been broken and fractured at this point in courtship.

If no forward movement is made, couples eventually find themselves at an impasse and go their separate ways. This separation not only brings heartache to the man and woman but the children and family members who have been involved with the year's long relationship. "Fortified" hearts and calloused attitudes begin to develop in both male and female, making it even harder for the next person to get in. That's why it is important to have clear understanding of what each person is looking for in the relationship and what outcome they desire to see. Men make sure you're not benefiting from her title of "Wifey" when you've only placed her at the level of MVP!***

(Back to the story)

Just like a good "Wifey" should, she's now fixing your dinner and packing your lunch. She washes your clothes and makes sure you're prepared for work. She's helping you manage your business affairs and even watches your children when you need a night out with the boys! She doesn't complain too much just occasionally asks when you will have time for her like you use to. Although a little irritated by her "demands" for you to spend a little more time with her, you ignore it for the "marriage itch" and continue on with life as usual. I mean, in your mind things are good right? You haven't given her a ring or promise of marriage, she's only doing the things a good woman and "wifey" should do.

It's her job to be understanding of your attitudes and be willing to put up with some of your not so good "habits." Cooking and cleaning and standing by her man is what a good wife does, right?

You know that she is "All In." You see how no other man can catch her attention, not even your boy with his wandering eyes who looks better than you and has more money than you too! She is faithful just the way you would want your wife to be. Cheating is not in her vocabulary! She truly is a "wife" for life and by the way you handle her, treat her, love on her and present her, you know this to be the TRUTH too! She's "Wifey" material, any man can see that! She's a good woman who handles her business and handles it well!

Your mom loves her, your kids adore her, even your friends respect what you guys have! Oh yes! She's "Wifey" material! It's apparent to all!

The sad thing is, she doesn't realize that you haven't quite made that commitment yet. Yes she's wonderful and has all the right attributes and characteristics of a great wife; however the title "wifey" is just that, a title. She's your MVP, the most valuable and needed member on your team. She's everything you've ever desired in a woman; why mess up a good thing with a ring?

The Journey to US continues....

He Put A Ring On It!
(Her)

Its been 5 years. You've played the "Wifey" role and are tired of playing house. Your baby-doll and green army man daydream died in your teenage years. You're a grown woman and you're ready for more!

You cook, you clean, and you wash dishes. You fold laundry, take care of his sick kids and even run errands for his mom because you love her. You've taken his bachelors pad and transformed it into a "home" all while raising and nurturing your own kids, helping with homework, paying bills at your own home, going to parent conference and working! You're doing it all but it seems to escape his attention.

You guys have attended other people's weddings and you continue to drop little hints but he seems fine with things "just as they are." He's says your his MVP, "Wifey" and number one supporter yet the walk down the "aisle of matrimony" continues to elude you. It's time for an ultimatum! Either you guys take the next step or despite the pain it will cause you, you'll get to stepping! You're tired of being the "cow" that gives the milk for free! It's time for him to purchase the whole "Kit and Caboodle!"

You prepare an amazing dinner, send the kids to "grandmas" for the night and rehearse your "speech" on how it's time to move forward. He comes home, dinner goes quite well. You guys joke, laugh and give each other little kisses as you repeatedly tell each other how much you love them!

You walk him over to the couch and begin to speak about your future together. You notice him get a little stiff but you plow ahead in hopes that he can see the wonderful future that you see! You pray inside that he would realize that you've truly been a "wife" faithful, loving and by his side! You remind him of how his mom continues to say, "Y'all need to go ahead and get married," and how his boys say, "You ain't never had a girl like her, you might as well go on and wife that one." You reason with him that it's just the next natural progression in a relationship that has been going on for so long but even after all that, your heart drops as you hear the words, "Why mess up a good thing?"

Your tears, your pleas and even the packing of your things seem to do nothing to break his resolve. He's not ready to move forward and you will no longer allow yourself to play the part of "Wifey." at this point in your life its ALL or nothing! Play time is over! You know you're a good woman and you remind him of that as you walk out of the door and out of his life......

Fast Forward 3 Weeks

For several days you cried yourself to sleep. He tried to call you and see you but by his conversation you knew that although he missed you, he still wanted to "play house" and because you know you deserve more you hang on to your dignity and tell him, "No, I want more. Go find someone who doesn't mind being "wifey" but never a wife."
His mom even calls and tries to convince you to come back.

She understands your stance but tells you that it will happen "one day" just don't give up on him. You think to yourself, I didn't give up on him, he gave up on us! You continue on with your life knowing that one day the pain will subside and you will be a-OK!

(side note)*A real man knows when he's messed up royally! After lying to himself that he'll be OK, he's not going to allow anyone to "force" him into marrying them; reality soon sets in and he realizes that his "MVP" was actually "Wife to be." determined to get his life back in order, he does what deep down inside, he's known he should have done years ago....he goes and buys a RING! (Back to the story)

Your life, although not great, is starting to get better. You can start to see a tiny glimmer of light at the end of the tunnel when out of nowhere he appears on your doorstep! Surprised but still filled with resolve you walk by but because you're a lady and still in love with him, you let him in.

As you turn around with an attitude, ready to yell, "Why are you here?!" your words get caught in your throat as you see him on his knees, ring in hand and hear those melodious words come from his lips, "Baby I Love You. Will You Marry Me?"

Of course you said "Yes!" after all these years he finally put a ring on it!

Let The Process of US begin!

Wifey Material
(Him)

Its been 5 years. She's played "Wifey" all this time and you know that she's tired of playing house. She wants more! And why shouldn't she? She cooks, she cleans, and she washes dishes.

She folds your laundry, takes care of your sick kids and even run errands for your mom because of her love her. Your "MVP" has taken your sorry bachelors pad and transformed it into a "home" all the while she's raising and nurturing her own kids, paying bills at her own home, and working! As exhausting as all that is, she still manages to find time for you! Oh yes, she's most definitely "Wifey Material!"

Fear has you stuck! What if you put a ring on it and she changes? With all the women out there, what if she's not the one? What if you can't live of up to the hype of a "good husband?" but you can't share those fears with her so you convince yourself that "pet" names such as MVP, and "Wifey" are enough to show her how much you love her and how much she means to you! You try to push away the fact that you know she wants to walk down the "aisle of matrimony." So you ignore her hints in hopes that she will soon get tired and stop asking.

Finally you get hit with an ultimatum! You knew it was coming! Either you guys are going to take the next step or she will get to stepping!

When you came home and saw the roses, candles and mouthwatering dinner, you knew it was time to face the music.

You guys joked, laugh and give each other little kisses. You told her how much you loved her and she told you the same! If only the night could have ended there! When she walked you over to the couch, you steeled yourself for the speech that was sure to follow.

She grabs your hand and begins to speak about your future together. Hopefully she didn't notice you stiffen at her words. When she continues to plow ahead talking about your wonderful future you sigh in relief! She didn't notice. (*Yes she did*).

You hear her talking about how she been faithful as a "wife," loving, caring and how she has stood by your side! She reminds you of how your mom (*traitor*) is always saying, "*Y'all need to go ahead and get married,*" and how your boys (*traitors*) continue to say, "*You ain't never had a girl like her, you might as well go on and wife that one.*"

She reasons that marriage is the natural progression in a relationship where two people love each other and have been together for so long! She tells you, "No man buys the "cow" if he continues to get the milk for FREE!"

Tears are running down her face as she pleads with you to do right by her but she can tell that her words have fallen on deaf ears when you stupidly utter, "Why mess up a good thing?"

Even though you hated to see her packing her things, you stayed determined in not breaking your resolve. You're not ready to move forward and she no longer wants play the part of "Wifey" she wants to be a WIFE! She wants ALL or nothing! Play time for her is over! You know she's a good woman and she reminds you of that fact as she walks out of the door and out of your life......

For three weeks she's refused your calls and your attempts to see her! No matter how cleverly you try to disguise your words she knows you still want to "play house." She deserves more and you know it but your fears of the future continue to plague you. You miss her so much you even had your mom call her to try and convince her to come back.

You understand why she left but why she gotta be so stubborn?! Things were good! There was no need to mess up what you had! A ring and a piece of paper is not what it's all about, it's about LOVE! (*You convince yourself yet?*)
Before you'll be forced to marry, you'll be by yourself and that settles that!

***(side note)*A real man knows when he's messed up royally! After lying to himself that he'll be OK, he's not going to allow anyone to "force" him into marrying them; reality soon sets in and he realizes that his "MVP" was actually "Wife to Be." Deep down inside, he knows what he needs to do. In fact he's known it all along. He has to marry this one! He goes and buys a RING! He's going to get his GOOD THING back!! *** **(Back to the story**

This will not be the "Fish" that got away! You refuse to start back over in hopes of finding someone like her! Armed with a ring and roses you go to her house and wait until she gets home from work! If you had to wait on her doorstep all night you were willing! Your pride got you into this trouble; your humility is going to get you out!

When she pulled up you could tell she was surprised to see you but she had to keep her "face" on. She walked right by you but you could that she was STILL in LOVE with you! (*Yessssss!*)

Because she's a lady she allowed you to come in but you knew that once she closed the door she was going to let you have it! No worries, you had the cure for what ails her! This one here is "Wifey" material! She has what it takes to walk by your side! She's shown it year after year after year and now it's time to man up and turn her D.R.E.A.M into reality!

She puts her stuff down and turns around attitude all on her face, but she froze, her words caught in her throat as you bended on one knee, ring in hand, and LOVE in your heart say the words that she has so desperately been waiting to hear, "Baby I Love You. Will You Marry Me?"

Of course she said "Yes!" as she burst into tears falling into your arms. After all these years you finally overcame your pride and fear, your sir put a ring on it!

Let The Process of US begin!

Engagement
marks the end of a whirlwind romance and the beginning
of an eternal love story.

~Author Unknown

I am my Beloved's, and my Beloved is Mine
~ Song of Solomon 2:16

Wives submit yourselves to your own husbands as unto the Lord.
~ Ephesians 5:22

I have found the one whom my soul loves
~ Song of Solomon 3:4

Bridal Shower
(Her)

Just like the little "Tea parties" you held as a little girl, your guest seated around your little table, YOU ARE THE CENTER OF ATTENTION! ALL eyes are on you!

The very thing you shared with your dolls is actually about to go down! You're about to receive your "dowry" from your girls. They're going to shower you will all kinds of gifts! It's SHOW TIME!

"Attention! Attention!" I'm engaged! Look at my ring! He asked me to marry him! It's time to PAR-TAY!! TONIGHT IT'S ALL ABOUT ME!!!

BUT...

After all of the gifts, squeals of delight, funny games, food and drink; after the sexy lingerie has been packed up, marriage advice given and the last guest leaves, you alone stand face to face with the realization that very soon you will be a "Mrs."

The countdown to the end of the ME season has commenced!

I am my Beloved's, and my Beloved is Mine
~ Song of Solomon 2:16

*Husbands, love your wives, even as Christ also loved
the church, and gave himself for it*
~ Ephesians 5:25

I have found the one whom my soul loves
~ Song of Solomon 3:4

Bachelor Party
(Him)

Man you finally did it! Time for the old ball and chain! You did good on that ring! You can't believe you're actually engaged! It's time to PAR-TAY! TONIGHT IT'S ALL ABOUT ME!

You sit back and smile enjoying the bravado, music and friends.

BUT...

After all your boys leave, advice given and jokes done; you alone stand face to face with the realization that very soon you will be the husband of a WIFE! The happiness, fear and weight of it begins to set in...

The countdown to the end of the ME season has commenced!

Here Comes The Bride
(Her)

Here comes the bride all dressed in white.
None can compare to her beautiful sight.
Look at how she glows let heaven and earth know
This union will last til eternity row.

Gentle is her walk as winds to the sail.
Wondrous is she who hides behind the Vail.

Here comes the bride all dressed in white.
God's gift to the groom, she's his perfect delight.
Joined on one accord by heaven above.
Blessed are those who witness the alliance of love.

Adorned in elegance every step she takes,
The eyes of the groom and the room she captivates.

Love was made for two- God put us both together and
I was made for you- a match made in Heaven and
How I love you too- blessed is your virtue and
Soon as I see you baby, I'm going to ask you
Will you marry me?
Please/will you say I do.

~Richard Wagner

I wonder if we knew what the words of the "wedding march" we stepped to actually said, how many women and men, would have taken their marriage VOWS more seriously?

The song speaks to the purity of a woman's heart, soul and love (all dressed in white).

It talks of how she glows due to her impending union and that both Heaven and earth are witnessing this momentous occasion! When God recorded this union in Heaven it was meant to LAST FOREVER!

Gentle is her walk as wind to the sail means this woman knows how to win her husband by her meek and gentle conversation (*1 Peter 3:1*). She's a wondrous sight to see when she knows how to "lower her tongue" in submission and respect (vail) to her husband. There is nothing more beautiful than a woman behind the vail and the Veil (she gets in the presence of God so that she doesn't "get in her husband's face!") In this position she is Ezer Kenegdo-lifesaver, nurturer, power and strength! She is the HELP who walks alongside her husband! Women, once the vail is raised, stay behind the Veil!

She's a *gift* given by God, a good thing that brings favor. His fountains blessed as he delights and rejoices in her (*Proverbs 5:18*).

They are an alliance, a union formed for the purposes of God.

Elegant and captivating she catches her grooms' eyes, a match made in Heaven, no man can divide!

Yes Dear Bride, all eyes are on you. Just know your season of ME is up right after you say "I Do."

I have found the one whom my soul loves
~ Song of Solomon 3:4

For this cause shall a man leave his father and mother, and shall be joined unto his wife, and they two shall be one flesh.
~ Ephesians 5:31

Husbands, love your wives, even as Christ also loved the church, and gave himself for it.
~ Ephesians 5:25

Fluttering Heart and Sweaty Palms
(Him)

Sorry gentlemen, but there is no song for you. You must patiently wait as the one who stole your heart makes her way to you.

You are the "bridegroom" the husband of the bride. Although the ceremony is about you both, still she remains the center of attention. She is your delight, the gift given you by God. She is your "help meet," YOUR Mrs., YOUR bride!

All the nervous laughter, fluttering heart and sweating palms dissipate as the doors open revealing your Queen. You knew she was beautiful but nothing could prepare you for the vision you are a seeing!

She's radiant, glowing, and wondrous beyond belief and she's yours, all yours all other suitors can now take a seat!

Here comes the bride all dressed in white.
God's gift to YOU, she's perfectly your delight.
Joined on one accord by heaven above.
Blessed are those who witness the alliance of love.

Yes she's your Bride, all eyes on you. Will your cry, shed a tear as she walks towards you? She's just about there, she's made it to you, your season of ME is up right after you say "I Do."

Love may be blind but Marriage is a real Eye-opener
~Author Unknown

This Just Got Real!

The nostalgia is over.

The honey moon was great!! Love all in the air! The newly wed Mr. and Mrs. are filled with an "US against the world" mentality!

While settling into their new lives together, most couples never envisioned increasing mortgages, high bills, sickness, being laid off of work, back to back pregnancies, "in-law" issues, their mates suddenly becoming "successful" and in demand in business, spending more time away from home then at home.

Never do they envision getting "sick and tired" of routine life, coming home to the same issues, spouse and kids. Temptation from the opposite sex never entered their minds, all they could see was a lifetime of "US," now this "US" is being challenged by life and time!

Gone are the times of running back to your own pad. You are now in the same household; two different personalities, temperaments, mindsets and behaviors trying to merge into one or at least some kind of amicable compromise.

The rose colored glasses have now come off, you can see clearly now the fog of love is gone. Things are crystal clear,

IT JUST GOT REAL!

Wait a Minute!! What About ME?!
(Him and Her)

Wait a minute, what about me! Before marriage I did what I wanted, when I wanted, how I wanted! I could go out whenever I wanted and stay out as late as I wanted! I could leave town when I wanted and I didn't have to answer to anybody!

(Him) Now I'm on my way home and I get sent a grocery list, a to-do list and a "we need to talk list!" When I finally do get home what do I walk into...toys, clothes and issues! What about me time? What about relaxation time? I didn't know I signed up for this! Where was this in our vows? What about me?

(Her) What?! He wants dinner every night, like he can't order out sometimes?! He has got to be kidding! I work 8 to 10 hours every day just like him! How dare he think I'm supposed to come home prepare dinner, fix it, and put it at his feet!!! What about me? Why can't he fix me dinner? I didn't sign up to be no maid!

(Him) I can't even rest when I get home! She wants to talk to me about the bills and talk to me about the kids! She gets mad because I didn't recognize her new hairstyle (*she always gets her hair done! It's pretty just like all the other times!*) Her car needs an oil change, its dirty and needs washing; you trying to tell me you can't make an appointment at the repair shop or run your car through the DRIVE THROUGH wash?! I use to go shoot pool with the boys, now all of a sudden it's a problem!

(Her) I can't get one night out with the girls?! He's tripping about keeping the kids like I had them by myself! And what's this "asking" all about? Why I gotta "ask" if I can go out with the girls and "ask" if I can go minister? I'm not a kid! I'm a grown woman! I've always made my own decisions! Kids get permission, not grown women! I didn't sign up for this!

(BOTH) WHAT ABOUT ME?!

A strong marriage requires two people who choose to love each other even on those days when they struggle to like each other.

~ Dave Willis

Hitting the Scriptures

All scripture is given by inspiration of God, and is profitable for doctrine, for reproof, for **correction, for instruction** in righteousness.

~ 2 Timothy 3:16

1 Corinthians 13
(Love Doesn't Look Out For SELF)

1 Corinthians 13, the "Love" chapter of the Bible. We have heard it preached, probably shared it with others but have you ever thought about it in terms of MARRIAGE! This passage of scriptures (*specifically verse 5*) helped me to DIE to me! I became the wife I *thought* I was after the Holy Spirit checked me and told me it's no longer about me!

Verse 1 says: *"Thou I speak with the tongues of men and of angels, and have not charity (love), I am become as sounding brass, or a tinkling cymbal."* In other words ladies and gentlemen, I don't care how much you "hababo shata," wanna-buy-a-hondai, and tie-my-bowtie-untie-my-bowtie," if you are not operating in love you are empty and irritating! Your spouse could care less how much you preach at church or how many awards you win at the office, if that same enthusiasm and passion isn't shown at home for your mate and family, you really haven't accomplished anything! Your spouse if your FIRST priority!

Verse 2: *"And though I have the gift of prophecy, and understand all mysteries, and all knowledge; and though I have all faith, so that I could remove mountains, and have not charity, I am nothing!"* Everybody is impressed with your abilities! You are a problem solver for everyone! The "go to" person when people need help! And man can you pray!

Everyone is blown away by your person, everyone that is, except your mate! To them you ain't NOTHING! (*I didn't say it, the Bible did!)*

Verse 3: *"And though I bestow all my goods to feed the poor, and though I give my body to be burned, and have not charity (love), it profiteth me nothing."* You're running money to your mama, your daddy, your sister, brother and friends! You stay up late worried about other people's kids, when your kids are suffering at home! You work from dusk to dawn only home long enough to eat, sleep, and then leave again. Your family profits off you, your friends profit off of you, even your job and ministry profit off of you! The problem with this is the one you pledged your love and fidelity to in front of God and a whole bunch of witnesses receives NO LOVE from you! You take it for granted that they will always be there! You assume they will see how "wonderful" you are and how needed you are." Surely your mate understands how important you are and how much people rely on you, it's not like you're not going to "make time" for them sometime soon.

While you become a "hero" to everyone else, your spouse is becoming a "villain" to you. The tender touches and kisses stop, date nights are rare and the love making has been put on "lock!" sweet nothings whispered in the ears have now become yells of bitterness and hatred. Hot nights spent in your lovers embrace has now turned into the cold shoulder of "edge of the bed" sleeping. All that you do for others profits you NOTHING if LOVE LACKS in the home!

Verse 4: *"Charity (love) suffereth long, and is kind; charity (love) envieth not; charity (love) vaunteth not itself, is not puffed up. "* here's where the "fun" begins... even in the midst of all the above listed wrong, LOVE must continue to be the banner over your marriage and household! LOVE suffers long, means that it is PATIENT even in the most difficult of times and it still remains KIND! Love doesn't hold grudges, keep a score card of wrong doings nor is love prideful (all about me), arrogant (all about me) or high minded (all about me).

You've heard the saying "two wrongs don't make it right" so why do you resort to passive aggressive behavior when you don't get what you want? Why is the "D" word (divorce) easily thrown out there when you don't get your way? Yes, you should expect love, attention and affection from your spouse; those things should be given without question but what happens when they aren't? Does that mean you have permission to walk away? No ma'am and No sir! What this means is it is time to dig in and get dirty! It means DYING TO SELF AND LIVING UP TO YOUR VOWS ANYWAY! This is the part of the "for better or for worse" part! It means learning how to hit your knees in prayer and then getting up to LOVE your spouse in spite of! Oh yes, this dying is no punk! It will get the jelly out of you!

Don't get me wrong, I'm not advocating that you stay in a physically abusive relationship; God didn't call us to be a punching bag! What I am talking about is this, "although God showed you the warning signs before you got married and even "spoke" to you via friends, sermon or even television" you still walked into that marriage eyes wide shut now you have to do the work to make it WORK!

Verse 5: *"Doth not behave itself unseemly, **seeketh not her own**, is not easily provoked, thinketh no evil;* this verse right here is the one that the Holy Spirit used to "pop" my "all about me" bubble! I remember complaining in my head about how much my husband sleeps. I thought to myself, *"he's always working, then he's studying or praying, he eats his dinner and off to sleep he goes!"* at this time I was upset because I wanted to go out to eat and to the movies and he didn't want to go because he was tired. This wasn't my first time complaining in my head about what my husband doesn't do for me and I guess the Holy Spirit had enough of my complaining! I felt right in my funky attitude as I sat on the couch, arms folding, mumbling under my breath! I didn't care about the fact that my husband could barely keep his eyes open to talk to me and that at that time he was working almost 16hrs every day! All I knew is that I wanted what I wanted and I didn't appreciate the fact that he couldn't force himself to stay up and take me out! Immediately I heard the Spirit of the Lord say, *"LOVE seeketh not its own"* all my inner grumbling stopped immediately! In shame I lowered my head and said Lord forgive me. Instantly compassion hit my heart for my husband as I truly RECOGNIZED the hard work he was putting in just to make sure that I was taken care of. He was wearing himself out to make sure our lights didn't get turned off, our bills were paid, our kids and grandchildren could have if they ever needed us and all I was worried about was ME.

This correction changed my whole life and perspective about marriage. IT'S NOT ABOUT YOU! It's about the US you became when you said "I Do."

Think about it ladies, when you were single (or if your contemplating marriage now) one of your prayers besides him being a good man (a man who loves God), and a faithful man was that he have a JOB! So now that you have a good and faithful man, why has this job you required him have become such an issue? Far too many women have found themselves in the bed of adultery because their husbands "worked too much" yet it's the very thing that you asked for. Why not compliment him on the way he takes care of home? Why not go out of your way to make your home a place of refuge and peace for him instead of a war zone of female hormones? Why not take your desire for time with your husband to the Lord and ask Him to speak to your husbands' heart about your desire to spend intimate time with him? I guarantee you it works! When I stopped complaining and started praying, God moved on my husband's heart. One day he came to me and said, "babe, I know I spend a lot of time at work but this weekend you and I are going to go out." he went on to say that the Lord told him that he needed to spend more time with me. I just smiled like a fat kid in a candy store!

My arguing and complaining didn't move him, prayer to our Father did! I submitted to his mission for our house and he submitted to the will of the Father concerning US!

Love doesn't seek her own! Love doesn't provoke! Love doesn't think evil towards another!

Gentlemen, the same holds true for you too! Just because you are the "head of the house" doesn't mean you aren't to take your wife's thoughts, opinions and emotions into consideration!

You knew when you dated and married her that she loved to go shopping, she loved getting her hair and nails done and she LOVED spending time with YOU! You made her feel special, protected, wanted and desired! When you stop the intimacy (stop seeing INTO her) she no longer feels lovely, wanted or needed. I guarantee she appreciates your hard work but know that when all that hard work crowds her out, she feels your job (or someone in that job) has become your mistress! Love doesn't seek its own! When you can go home early, GO HOME! Don't allow the overtime to divide your marriage! If you've made hanging out with your boys more important than spending time with her you make her feel unloved and unappreciated! When you put your mama before her, you have no made her play "second string" in your orchestra and after a while she's going to start playing "out of tune." Love seeks not its own!
You can't treat your cars better than you treat your wife! You will wash your car weekly, shine it weekly, vacuum it weekly and make sure it gets complete tune ups on schedule yet your wife can't get you to wash her with your love, let alone the Word of God! She needs "tune ups" too and not on a schedule! Sometimes she (and women he) needs it nightly if you get my drift!

Marriage is WE not ME! It's about two people learning how to become ONE!

Ephesians 5:21says, *"Submitting yourselves one to another in the fear of God."*
Verse 33 reads, *"Nevertheless let every one of you in particular so love his wife even as himself; and the wife see that she reverence her husband."*

What does submission really mean? Apostle Cal Lawanson (Kansas City, Mo.) explained it this way, *Sub-* means under, *mission-* means the purpose of a person. In marriage you bring yourselves *under* the *purpose* of your mate! In other words by you submitting to the purpose of your mate you cause them to be lifted up! You have to get under something to RAISE IT! So now her dreams become your dreams and his aspirations become your aspirations! You literally become ONE in purpose and intent! The two have now become ONE! LOVE SEEKS the betterment of the other!

Verse 6-7: Love, *"Rejoiceth not in iniquity, but rejoiceth in truth;* Love, *"Beareth all things, believeth all things, hopeth all things, endureth all things."* Love does not rejoice, get happy, and giggle inside when something bad happens to your spouse. There is no "I told you so" mentality! Love bears things that would be easy to walk out on! Love believes when your spouse says, *"I had to work late"* and doesn't automatically assume your spouse is cheating! Love hopes against hope and weathers the storms of life together! Love endures times of financial crisis, health crisis, problems with children, loss of employment, garnishments, erectile dysfunction, weight gain, etc...

Verse 8a: ***"LOVE NEVER FAILS...."***

Genesis 2:18
(Help Meet)

"And the Lord God said, It is not good that the man should be alone; I will make him an help meet for him."

Men, if you could have been fruitful with the ability to multiply by yourself (Ch.1, vss. 27-28) and if you could have decorated and cleaned your house (Ch.2, vs. 15) and if you knew how to go into the kitchen and pick out the right ingredients and seasonings, all by yourself, God would never have had to make woman in verse 18! You needed some help!

Vs. 18: *And the Lord God said, it is not good that the man should be alone; I will make him an help meet for him."*

Genesis Ch. 1 verse 27 tells us that God had already created man (male and female) in His image and likeness, yet if you notice, He was only working with man at first! Not only do I believe this was because of man's headship but also because men (according to science) its takes you guys longer to "get it!" He had to give you guys a "running start" before He formed the woman. (*It's ok to laugh, it won't kill you!*)

Your job men (according to Ch.2, vs. 15) was to dress and keep the Garden of Eden (home) so please understand it's not just the woman's duty. You were the original house cleaner. Verse 19 says that God brought the animals he formed from the ground to Adam for him to name and whatever Adam called them, that was their name! Every created animal had someone except Adam.

God seeing Adam alone (as well as his decorating, cleaning and naming skills) decided to give the man some help. Verse 21 tells us that God caused Adam to fall into a deep sleep and then he took one of his ribs, closed up the wound and made woman from it (vs. 22).

When Adam woke up, he saw the gift that God had brought to him. He said, *"This is bone of my bones, and flesh of my flesh: she shall be called Woman, because she was taken out of Man."* He instantly knew she was a part of him!

Husbands, your wife was created by God to walk alongside you; that's why she was taken from your side. She is not a slave, a doormat or a "silent partner" she's your "help meet" the Ezer, that God has gifted to you to help you dress, tend, decorate and push your vision! She was given an assignment to! God blessed **them** and told **them** to be fruitful and multiply and replenish the earth. He told **them** to subdue it and to have dominion over every living thing! You both were given an assignment at your creation, she is a part of you; LOVE HER with that understanding! Ephesians 5:25, *"Husbands LOVE your wives, even as Christ loved the church, and gave himself for it."*
You are to love your wives as your own bodies. The bible says if you love your wife you love yourself! You don't hate yourself; you nourish yourself and cherish yourself. That's the same way you are to nourish and cherish your wife! (*Ephesians 5:28-29*).

Wives, you were taken out of your husband's side to walk beside him, not to lead him like your puppy or child! Eve took the lead and look what happened! Let your husband take you under his arms and protect you, lead you, guide you and LOVE you!
So many women have had to raise children on their own and pay their own bills so long that they no longer see nor honor the position and responsibility of the husband.

RESPECT the fact that he has provided a home for you (I don't care if it was your home that he moved into) he's there now, he's the head! Ephesians 5:22-24, *"Wives, submit yourselves unto your own husbands, as unto the Lord."* why is it that you can submit to the pastor, submit to your boss but fight against yourself (your husband)?
"For the husband is the head of the wife, even as Christ is the head of the church: and is the savior of the body." the husband is the head, he doesn't need a drill sergeant or another mother, he already has one.
"Therefore as the church is subject unto Christ, so let the wives be subject to their own husbands in everything."
If you're fixing dinner for the pastor, your mama, your grown kids and everyone else yet get an attitude when your husband wants dinner, you ma'am are out of order and your "habasata"(your tongue speaking) means nothing if you neglect the order of God.

Husbands please know that your wife is more than just your "Dinner Server," "Eye Candy," and "Bed Warmer." She is a gift presented by God to you! The one called to walk alongside and help you! She is YOU! The two saith HE are become ONE!

Song of Solomon
(I am my Beloved's)
Song of Solomon 2:16 "My beloved is mine, and I am his..."

King Solomon was a very wise man. In fact the bible states that there was none wiser before him neither will there be any wiser after him. Wisdom is what he is known for. When reading Song of Solomon I also realize that King Solomon is also known for the fact that he liked to get some! (*Again, it's okay to laugh people!)*

The marriage bed is NOT the place for attitudes, arguments, work stress, and 15 headaches and 3 cycles every month! It's the place for intimacy!

In your single years, you couldn't wait to get married so you could get some every night. Now that you're married and your D.R.E.A.M has become a reality, you realize that marriage is more than just sex! However, no matter how hard it may get to like each other, sex is NOT a weapon to be used against your mate! WITHHOLDING is of the devil!

1 Corinthians 7:5 (NLT) says, *"Do not deprive each other of sexual relations, unless you both agree to refrain from sexual intimacy for a limited time so you can give yourselves more completely to prayer. Afterward, you should come together again so that Satan won't be able to tempt you because of your lack of self-control."*
Don't set your spouse up for failure by putting a lock on sexual intimacy! If you didn't want to have sex, you shouldn't have gotten married!

In a world full of temptation, don't let your pride or selfishness be the cause of your spouse's infidelity! You're not going to agree on everything and you are most definitely going to get on each others nerves but with that being said, do not withhold the cookies and do not sheath your sword!

1 Corinthians 7:2-4 (NIV) *"But since sexual immorality is occurring, each man should have sexual relations with his **own wife** and each woman with her **own husband.** The husband should fulfill his marital duty to his wife, and likewise the wife to her husband. The wife does not have authority over her own body but yields it to her husband. In the same way, the husband does not have authority over his own body but yields it to his wife."*

There is an enemy out there, a tempter who wants to see marriages destroyed, families decimated and self-esteem bull dozed, therefore don't give him the ammunition to destroy your marriage! It is your marital duty to fulfill the sexual desires of your spouse! Yield (submit) yourself to their desire for you, don't allow anger or pride to get in the way. Besides sexual intimacy with your spouse isn't just a duty, ITS FUN!!
Sexual intimacy keeps the bond and unity of "Oneness" strengthened! The less you become one; the easier it is to divide the two! Why do you think it is that as soon as your spouse gets on your nerves, the immediate "flesh" response is to withhold?
It's because the enemy knows that as soon as he causes you to despise each other, not desire each other and defraud each other; he has successfully divided your house and a house divided against itself will not stand!

Proverbs 5:15-18 (NIV) *"Drink water from your own cistern, and running water from your own well. Should your springs overflow in the streets, your streams of water in the public squares?* **Let them be yours alone, never to be shared with strangers.** *May your fountain be blessed, and may you rejoice in the wife of your youth. A loving doe, a graceful deer—may her breasts satisfy you always, may you ever be intoxicated with her love. Why, my son, be intoxicated with another man's wife? Why embrace the bosom of a wayward woman? For your ways are in full view of the LORD, and he examines all your paths."*

Get drunk on each others love! Wives let your breast satisfy your husband! Let him get "wasted" on your scent and your love! This is the man you said "I Do" too! Husbands be intoxicated by your wife's passion, the hills and valleys that make up her body! This is the wife of your youth! The wife you pledged your fidelity to! Let her breast satisfy you ALWAYS!

You are your Beloved's and your Beloved's is yours! The three fold cord of marriage is you, God and your spouse! What God put together let no man (woman) bring asunder!

Malachi 2:13-14
(Don't act surprised!)

"Another thing you do: You flood the LORD's altar with tears. You weep and wail because he no longer looks with favor on your offerings or accepts them with pleasure from your hands. You ask, "Why?" It is because the LORD is the witness between you and the wife of your youth. You have been unfaithful to her, though she is your partner, the wife of your marriage covenant." (NIV)

You may fool man but you can never fool God! Far too often I find myself counseling couples who for one reason or another find themselves dealing with the betrayal of an unfaithful spouse. You can see the pain and even the void behind the eyes of the betrayed and although they are sitting there in counseling, their heart has already left the building.

Please understand that God who sits high and looks low witnesses every unfaithful act performed against your spouse. Just because business still seems to be going great or you can still write and preach a sermon that has the church "going wild" doesn't mean Gods hand of favor is still on you! Remember, Samson's strength had already left him and he knew it not! Intellect in business and the gift to write and orate is the only thing keeping an unfaithful spouse afloat! The bible declares that gifts and callings are without repentance. In other words, you can still operate with no anointing and no favor!

The Covenant of Marriage represents and is symbolic of Christ and the Church (His Bride). Jesus is forever faithful to us even when we're unfaithful! He continues to woo us even when we constantly run to our former lovers!

How dare you think that you can flirt with the secretary at work, arrange "hook ups" during the lunch hour, meet your lover at a hotel (*although you told your wife you were working overtime*) come home and ignore your wife (*having your sexual needs met by another*) and still think God is going to continue to hear your prayers and bless the work of your hands? YOU MUST DIE TO YOU! Your wife, who is your partner in life and help meet, deserves your fidelity! It's easy to "excuse" your actions by saying she gained weight or you were under a lot of stress or your wife doesn't understand you or any other number of reasons you give yourself for cheating but when you get through with the excuses YOU'RE STILL WRONG! DIE TO YOUR EXCUSES! DIE TO YOUR SELFISH WAYS! DIE TO YOUR SELFISH DESIRES! Remember, LOVE SEEKS NOT ITS OWN! Cheating is the easy way out!

1 Peter 3:7 *"Likewise, ye husbands, dwell with them according to knowledge, giving honour unto the wife, as unto the weaker vessel, and as being heirs together or the grace of life; that your prayers be not hindered."*

When you dishonor your wife you effectively shut down your prayer life! Don't act surprised when you see your business decreasing, your anointing diminished and your ministry stalled! You decided to step out! God don't bless mess! Until you repent your prayers are basically hitting the ceiling and bouncing back to you! Husbands, DIE to your unrealistic expectations of your wives! DIE to your egotistical view of yourself and DIE to the temptation of the seductress! Falling is easy, Fighting is courageous!

Women, I hope you didn't think you were going to get off that easy! You need to learn how to DIE too! Not every man is the cheater in marriage, sometimes it's you beautiful "Gifts!"

Proverbs 2:11-17 *"Discretion will protect you, and understanding will guard you. Wisdom will save you from the ways of wicked men, from men whose words are perverse, who have left the straight paths to walk in dark ways, who delight in doing wrong and rejoice in the perverseness of evil, whose paths are crooked and who are devious in their ways. Wisdom will save you also from the adulterous woman (*or you becoming one*), from the wayward woman (*DIE TO YOU*) with her seductive words, who has left the partner of her youth (*DIE TO YOU*) and ignored the covenant she made before God."*

Ladies, you have to use discretion! Your baby's daddy has no business knowing what's going on in your home, with your husband and your sex life! Understand that "loose lips sink a whole bunch of ships!" Wisdom says just because you got mad at your husband or just because he hasn't touched you in weeks or just because you assume that he has "something going on" doesn't give you a right to take that other man's number! All those compliments and flattering words have dark, devious and perverse motives behind them! YOU'RE MARRIED, the enemy rejoices when you fall! Wisdom says don't meet up with your old lover! Don't fall for the "If I was your man" line! You don't need to lie down to get a raise whether in the office or at church!

Quit batting your eyes at men (that's seduction) quit "hitting the scene" with your single girlfriends, you ain't single! DIE TO THAT IT'S ALL ABOUT ME SPIRIT!

Just like with husbands, it's easy to "excuse" your actions by saying he doesn't spend enough time with me or he doesn't even compliment me anymore or he doesn't understand me and just takes me for granted or any other number of reasons you too are giving yourself to excuse your cheating but when it's all said and done, YOU'RE STILL WRONG! DIE TO YOUR EXCUSES! DIE TO YOUR SELFISH WAYS! DIE TO YOUR SELFISH DESIRES! Remember, LOVE SEEKS NOT ITS OWN! Cheating is the easy way out!

Don't be like the woman in Proverbs 30:20 who sleeps around on her husband and then claims it wasn't wrong. *"Such is the way of an adulterous woman; she eateth, and wipeth her mouth, and saith, I have done no wickedness."*

You ain't getting your prayers answered either! DIE to your unrealistic expectations of your husband! DIE to your overinflated view of yourself and DIE to the devious words of the tempter! Falling is easy, Fighting is courageous!

You want your marriage, house, ministry, business and family blessed? STAY FAITHFUL TO GOD AND YOUR SPOUSE!

Ephesians 5:31
(Mama's Boy/Daddy's Girl)
"For this cause shall a man leave his father and mother, and shall be joined unto his wife, and they two shall be one flesh."

Boyz 2 Men wrote a song called "A Song for Mama." We all get teary-eyed when we hear it as they sing about she taught him everything how she was there for him loving and caring for him. It goes on to say how she will always be the girl in his life for all times and how she is the Queen of his heart! They end the song by saying, "Loving you is like food to my soul..." how beautiful is that! Our moms are the ones who carried us, nurtured us and kissed our "hurts" to make them better! As great and wonderful as mothers are (and mine was the cream of the crop) don't let the "Queen of your heart" destroy the marriage with the woman of your dreams!

Respect for your parents does not mean permission granted for them to degrade your spouse! "Mama-nem" may or may not like or agree with the woman you chose to marry but they do have to respect her. She's your wife, the woman you vowed to "Honor and Keep...forsaking all others."

Husbands, your wife IS NOT your mama! She's not going to cook like her, clean like her, dress like her and in this day and time she's probably not going to serve like her (barefoot, pregnant and in the kitchen!) Don't drive a wedge between your family and your wife by running to mama and "telling on" your wife. Your allegiance is with your wife, remember LEAVE AND CLEAVE!

What your mom did for you and how she raised you was good for her and her household but she doesn't have the right to force her parenting skills on your wife. This is not to say that she can't make suggestions or offer help if she sees it needed but there still must be respect for the woman of your house! Always honor your mother and father but remember there are still some boundaries that they can't cross. You two are ONE; let no man bring it asunder, not even mama!

Ladies, while I know that made you cheer you too can't allow family to come between your marriage! Your husband IS NOT your Daddy! Quit trying to make him fill the void your daddy left behind whether good or bad! Your dad may have been your hero, a great dad who read you bed times stories and came to your rescue every time you needed him! Or maybe your daddy was an absentee father who you rarely ever saw and he never attended any of your birthday parties. Don't make your husband try to live up to the hype of "Hero Dad" neither destroy his every effort because of "Villain Dad."
Quit running to daddy for money every time there's a financial stress in your marriage! Your husband doesn't need your daddy to come to the rescue! Let your husband solve the problem, that is what he is designed and hard wired to do! Running to daddy only belittles the worth of your husband in your families eyes and causes your husband to feel "less than" because in his eyes, you don't believe in him.

Your marriage is between you and your husband. Leave "Mama-nem" out of your business!

1 Peter 3
(Stop all that YELLING!)

"Likewise, ye wives, be in subjection to your own husbands; that if any obey not the word, they also may without a word, be won by the conversation of the wives; while they behold your chaste conversation coupled with fear."

Helen Reddy said, *"I am woman, hear me roar."* Many of you women have taken that so seriously that "Roaring" is all you know how to do! Stop all that YELLING! I don't care how loud you get; you will never make a man "do" what you want by yelling at him. If anything, you'll drive him from your bed, your house, your life.....

Proverbs 27:15-16 says, *"A continual dripping in a very rainy day and a contentious woman are alike. Whosoever hideth her hideth the wind, and the ointment of his right hand, which bewrayeth itself."*
The Message Bible says it like this, *"A nagging spouse is like the drip, drip, drip of a leaky faucet. You can't turn it off and you can't get away from it..."*
The New Living Translation says, *"A quarrelsome wife is as annoying as constant dripping on a rainy day. Stopping her complaints is like trying to stop the wind or trying to hold something with greased hands."*

Water constantly dripping in the sink is so irritating! You try to ignore it, you still hear it. You cover your ears, you guessed it, you still hear it! There is no rest until you get that faucet fixed!
How about water leaking from your ceiling ruining everything in its path or frustrating you with its rhythmic plop-plop-plop as it strikes the filling bucket or pot you placed under it!

Ugh! You yell into the air which does no good! That my dear friend is how YOU sound with all that devilish yelling! You start to sound like the teacher in the cartoons "Wan-wan-wan-wan-wan!" you are IRRA! Why not choose the "quiet road?" sometimes your silence says more than any word you could ever speak!

I remember earlier in my marriage when I would go off on my husband at the drop of a hat! My complaints always varied, "you didn't carry the groceries in right!" "Why are you only carrying two bags at a time? Get them all! You're making too many trips!" then I would proceed to go outside and show him how it's done! Or maybe I'd be in one of my "why are you chewing like that?!" "Who makes mashed potatoes crunch?!" kind of moods. Talk about IRRA! I got on my own nerves sometimes!

One day, in the middle of a tirade, the Lord literally told me to be quiet! He went on to explain to me that I wasn't so perfect either! How dare I talk to my husband like I was all that!" needless to say, I learned my lesson and learned how to shut my mouth! In doing so, something beautiful happened; my husband actually started listening to me. He would ask my input on things and we began to problem solve as a team! My husband didn't need me yelling and trying to be his mama, he needed a wife that he could trust with both his strengths and weaknesses and not degrade him for them.

I won my husband through my chaste conversation. *"Pleasant words are as an honeycomb, sweet to the soul, and health to the bones."* Proverbs 16:24

Yelling, cussing out and name calling only leads to separation! Proverbs 21:9, *"It is better to dwell in a corner of the housetop, than with a brawling woman in a wide house."* You will be all alone in that big beautiful house if you don't stop all that yelling. A little corner of the roof is better than a big bed and your contentious words! If the enemy of your marriage can keep you and your husband at each other's throat, he knows it won't be too long before one or both of you find solace elsewhere.
Words DO HURT. Words can DO DAMAGE. Words can BE DESTRUCTIVE! Use your words to build your mate not tear them down.

Husbands, constantly degrading your wife for weight gain only worsens the matter. Yelling at her because you can't yell at your boss is unfair. Ruling her with an iron fist and a blaring mouth is indicative of an insecure man. Heal each other with your words.
Words can HEAL. Words can EDIFY. Words can BUILD!

Husbands and wives, Let me leave you with a few nuggets.
1. Watch what you say AND how you say it.
2. Some things are better left unsaid.
3. Stop name calling
4. Avoid accusations and blaming
5. Let the past stay in the past
6. Leave threats out
7. Find a neutral corner and settle down before resuming heated disagreements.
8. DIE TO YOUR RIGHT TO BE RIGHT! Sometimes you have to take one for the TEAM!

Two words sealed you in marital covenant; use those two words to keep you there!

Tell your mate "I DO:"
-Love you
-Honor you
-Cherish you
-Need you
-Desire you
-Want you
-Believe in you

TIL DEATH DO US PART!

Conclusion

I believe that there is truly a direct, decisive and divisive attack being launched against the sanctity of marriage. At the same time I also believe that there are people who are ready willing and able to counter these attacks through prayer, determination and love.
Your spouse is not your enemy; your warfare is not against them. You two have a common enemy who is afraid of your UNITY! Unity brings agreement, Unity denotes strength and Unity makes possible the impossible!

Ecclesiastes 4:12 (NLT) encourages us that, *"A person standing alone can be attacked and defeated, but two can stand back-to-back and conquer. Three are even better, for a triple-braided cord is not easily broken."*

Husbands and wives, as long as you keep God first and learn how to DIE to the "Me" spirit, there is no force on earth that can come between you, God and your mate!

The spirit of "Me" runs at the first sign of adversity, hardship or crisis. The covenant of "US" declares WE are in this together! When you allow God to take the lead in your marriage and fight for you, *One can chase a thousand and two shall put ten thousand to flight*!

Send them devils of separation and divorce packing! Lock arms and fight! The two have BECOME ONE!

OTHER TITLES BY OCTAVIA STANDLEY

TALL, LIGHT AND HANDSOME
FROM HURT TO HEALING
UNCAP YOUR LIFE
INSPECTION IN THE HOUSE
SEX AND THE SAINTS
THE POWER OF POSITION LEADERSHIP MANUAL

If you are interested in booking Apostle Octavia Standley for your next Conference, Gathering or Seminar; please email all request to:

remnantministrieskc@gmail.com

or

pastorostandley@gmail.com

We look forward to hearing from you!

Made in the USA
Las Vegas, NV
05 June 2021